551.56   Vilardi, Debbie.
VIL   What makes a rainbow?
            (Science questions)

DATE DUE			

**ANNIE E VINTON ELEMENTARY
SCHOOL LIBRARY**
306 STAFFORD ROAD
MANSFIELD CENTER, CT 06250

WHAT MAKES A RAINBOW?

by Debbie Vilardi

Cody Koala

An Imprint of Pop!

popbooksonline.com

abdobooks.com

Published by Pop!, a division of ABDO, PO Box 398166, Minneapolis, Minnesota 55439. Copyright © 2019 by POP, LLC. International copyrights reserved in all countries. No part of this book may be reproduced in any form without written permission from the publisher. Pop!™ is a trademark and logo of POP, LLC.

Printed in the United States of America, North Mankato, Minnesota

082018
012019

THIS BOOK CONTAINS
RECYCLED MATERIALS

Cover Photo: iStockphoto
Interior Photos: iStockphoto, 1, 5 (top), 17; Shutterstock Images, 5 (bottom left), 5 (bottom right) 7, 8, 10–11, 12, 15, 19, 20

Editor: Meg Gaertner
Series Designer: Laura Mitchell

Library of Congress Control Number: 2018950120

Publisher's Cataloging-in-Publication Data

Names: Vilardi, Debbie, author.

Title: What makes a rainbow? / by Debbie Vilardi.

Description: Minneapolis, Minnesota : Pop!, 2019 | Series: Science questions | Includes online resources and index.

Identifiers: ISBN 9781532162152 (lib. bdg.) | ISBN 9781641855860 (pbk.) | ISBN 9781532163210 (ebook)

Subjects: LCSH: Rainbows--Juvenile literature. | Prisms--Juvenile literature. | Meteorological optics--Juvenile literature. | Children's questions and answers--Juvenile literature.

Classification: DDC 500--dc23

Hello! My name is

Cody Koala

Pop open this book and you'll find QR codes like this one, loaded with information, so you can learn even more!

Scan this code* and others like it while you read, or visit the website below to make this book pop.

popbooksonline.com/makes-a-rainbow

*Scanning QR codes requires a web-enabled smart device with a QR code reader app and a camera.

Table of Contents

Rainbows

A rainbow is a curved line of colors in the sky. Most rainbows happen after rain. Sunlight hits water drops at an angle. Beautiful colors appear.

Watch a video here!

Light

Light moves as a wave from the Sun. It hits objects on Earth. The objects **absorb** some of the light.

They **reflect** the rest of it.

Complete an activity here!

Light comes in different **wavelengths**. These are the colors that people see. Different objects absorb different wavelengths of light.

People do not see the light an object absorbs. People see the light that is reflected.

For example, a leaf is
green. The leaf reflects the
wavelength people see
as green.

Sunlight is made of white light. It appears colorless. But it contains wavelengths of all colors.

Chapter 3

Separating Colors

A glass **prism** can separate white light into different colors. Light enters a glass prism. The light bends. Each wavelength bends at a different angle.

Learn more here!

The light exits the prism. Each wavelength appears in a different line. People see bands of separate colors.

How a Prism Works

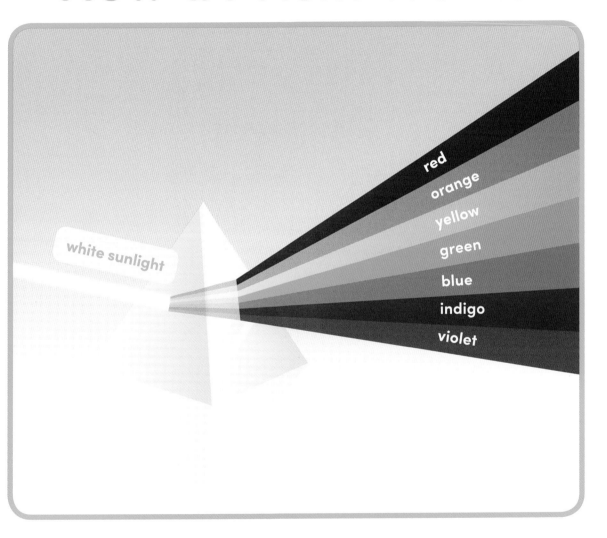

Chapter 4

Natural Prisms

Drops of water are natural prisms. Some drops hang in the air after a storm. Sunlight bends when it passes through the drops.

Rainbows also appear near waterfalls.

Learn more here!

The light reaches people's eyes. It appears as a rainbow.

Sometimes light reflects in the water drop twice. It makes a double rainbow.

Making Connections

Text-to-Self

Have you ever seen a rainbow? What did you think?

Text-to-Text

Have you read other books about weather topics? What new thing did you learn?

Text-to-World

People across the world enjoy rainbows. Why do you think people like them?

Glossary

absorb – to take in without giving back.

angle – the figure formed by two lines coming from the same point.

prism – a glass object with three sides that bends light and separates it into colors.

reflect – to bounce off an object.

wavelength – the distance from the highest point of one wave to the highest point of the next.

Index

Online Resources

popbooksonline.com

Thanks for reading this Cody Koala book!

Scan this code* and others like it in this book, or visit the website below to make this book pop!

popbooksonline.com/makes-a-rainbow

*Scanning QR codes requires a web-enabled smart device with a QR code reader app and a camera.